MW01138730

Narcissists &
Psychopaths
Prayer for Protection
Against Them

By

Liguori Ó Murchú

Queen of Angels Publishing

IMPORTANT

INTRODUCTION

I have it on good authority that, this page of my book is available for preview, (FREE) when considering whether or not, to buy this book on Amazon. And so since this is, a very important message in the book, I want you to know it; even if you go away without buying my book.

Maybe you believe in Prayer. Maybe the idea of Prayer is your last option. Or perhaps your done praying because evil seems to be winning. Or. Maybe you're just curious.

If you are not Christian, then I want you to consider using the following method as a scientific experiment.

First you must write down in a notebook your plan on how and when you mean to use the prayer. You must date this. You see when it works you will need to come back and log the results of your scientific experiment, that the prayer did indeed "work".

The prayer is the "Our Father". Now later in the book I will explain how to say the prayer according to particular situations. You will need to get a good handle on "Mental Prayer", and "Contemplative Prayer".

The definition of Prayer is "The raising of the mind and heart to God." We will look at how this is done. We will use the Bible for our inspiration and teaching.

For those of you who simply read this page and choose a different book: Please take this golden advice with you. Use the "Lord's Prayer," when dealing with the narcissist. Especially while they are face to face trying to destroy your life or lacerate your soul. Use it while THEY ARE TALKING. Speak it into YOURSELF.

Never, never tell them what you are doing. Why? Does the commander tell his war plans to the commander of the opposing forces? Of course he doesn't. We are at war with these emissaries of Satan. According to those who know; Satan cannot hear our prayers to God.

Definition of the Narcissist Personality Disorder

According to my social work training one of the highest skills of interaction between one human being and another is '*empathy*'. We have empathy when we understand other people's emotions – because we either have felt the same ourselves or we have the ability to perceive and understand the sufferings of others. Our response to our feelings of empathy is to treat the other person with kindness and dignity.

One of the core messages of Jesus Christ was to high-light, the need for 'empathy'. "*Do unto others as you would have them do unto you*". "*Love ye one another as I have loved you.*" "*Love your neighbour as yourself.*" These messages were so strong and resonated with such passion in the human heart that they actually formed Western Society with its hospitals, schools, Laws and Justice.

The film media and you-tube media recognise the soft hearts of most of the population and abound with stories that tug at the heart-strings.

But it must be said that at times we are all capable of not being empathetic. Sometimes, for whatever reason we deny others, our care and kindness.

Usually this is when we are under huge pressure because of our state in life. Money problems can cause us to be unaware of the needs of others. Marriage problems or the *pushing of our buttons* by others can render us devoid of sympathy for our fellow human beings.

The person who has a narcissist personality disorder does not have those 'heart strings', there is no *kindness* in them. They have no empathy or sympathy for others.

Science has proved that the psychopath and narcissist have different brain abnormalities from the normal person. MRI brain scans have proved that beyond a shadow of a doubt these predators are not *human*. This is not immediately apparent because they have learned to hide it so well.

Here are some of their 'attributes':
Grandiose sense of self-importance.
Preoccupied with a sense of power and desire for unlimited success. Expectations of special favours.
Manipulate others in order to get what they want.
Manipulate fear into others.
Use flattery to control others.
Without loyalty.

Liars and 'gaslighters'

Highly dangerous to others – men, women, children and even animals.

They are without a conscience.

This last is the most troublesome for me. When I do my nightly 'examination of conscience' and think back over my day and my behaviour; it is my conscience that points out the right and wrong that I have done. I try to recognise and work on my 'predominant fault'. I do my best to take full responsibility for my actions or inactions. I think this is pretty standard thinking for a Christian.

Not so the Narcissist and psychopath. He or she can do no wrong according to them. They will always blame others for any mistakes committed by them.

But they do know right from wrong because they will not steal in front of a police man. I know a pathetic Narcissist that says: "I too am a sinner." He always, always, turns his head fully sideways and away from me, when he says it!

I love the way they deny doing something no one has thought to blame them for. You suddenly think, 'I wouldn't even dream of accusing you of doing something like that." You are bewildered for a few moments then you see that vicious smile and *know* they did it. But you can never prove it and no one would believe you, if you tried to tell them.

When you first meet a Narcissist you may well love them with a passion beyond reason but when they have finished with you, there is a strong possibility that you will hate them with a cold blooded hatred that will shock and frighten you.

This is one of those times when you will need prayer.

Definition of the Psychopath

First a little disclaimer: For me the difference between a Narcissist and a Psychopath is how I feel on any given day. When deep seated anger gurgles up from my stomach into my brain; Narcissist are just plain Psychopaths. Please bear with me as throughout this text I will use both terms. If you have suffered from these types of people you will understand.

I suspect that the word Narcissist began to be used by professionals because the correct label of Psychopath spelled insane murderer. Psychopaths don't always murder but should be identified by society as highly dangerous people.

I have read articles written by self-diagnosed psychopaths who say that they do not need attention and respect. They like attention and respect but if they do *not* get it they are not overtly worried. They use attention and respect to get what they want. In other words attention and respect are not their goals in life but only (where necessary) a means to attain those goals.

Narcissist seek attention as their goal and are miserable without that attention because they are so taken up with themselves.   We all recognise the word narcissist as describing someone in love with themselves.

A Narcissist will feel hurt by rejection or public ridicule but a Psychopath has no such feelings. They do not feel the normal pain of rejection.

While Narcissist love to abuse and humiliate they hate it to be done to them.   Their abuse is more often revenge while the Psychopath enjoys thinking up ways to hurt others.

People equate the label psychopath, with serial killer behind bars.   But as a Christian you should know that the killing of the soul is a more heinous act and has far reaching consequences in eternity.

The Narcissism of the Psychopath will kill your soul – if you let them.   They are capable of driving you to despair. They can mesmerize you to take your own life.   They can make you hate others and through misguided loyalty to them - target those people.   They are often able to hypnotise you and get you to change your belief system.

I have heard it said that no one can be hypnotised to commit murder.   On the other hand I recently read that a study was done in 1961 in Yale University.   Apparently Mr Stanley Milgram carried out experiments which had very horrifying results. Mr Milgram's experiment demonstrated that 2 out of 3 people, that is most people, will perform a cruel action towards another person if instructed to do so by someone whom they regard as an authority figure. This shows that the majority of people are capable of doing an action they know to be wrong or against the Commandments of God even though they don't want to, if they are directed by a figure of authority or someone they hold in high esteem. Here is the internet link to watch a video of the experiments being carried out.

McLeod, S. A. (2007). The Milgram Experiment. Retrieved from **www.simplypsychology.org/milgram.html**

You cannot do wrong, even for what *you* think, is a good reason. So don't become what is termed a "flying monkey" on behalf of the evil person you admire or who has control over you.

When you escape from the clutches of the psychopath you need to be careful that the experience doesn't make you lose your faith in God, or worse still, blame God for your horrific experience.

There is a questionnaire used by professionals known as the Psychopathic Personality Inventory – Revised (PPI-R) test, it creates a total psychopathy score (PPI-R total) and studies such personality traits as:

Fearless dominance; self-centeredness; impulsivity and cold-heartedness.[i]

That should give us an idea of what we are dealing with.

The Satanically Possessed.

The satanically possessed? Well, they are a whole ballgame of their own. I have become entangled with three perfectly possessed people. Oh dear! Just thinking about it makes me short of breath.

Satanically possessed persons need not be psychopaths or narcissists or even nasty people. They can be nice people who have unwittingly invited in the oppression of an evil entity. Usually called a demon, the entity causes the person to do evil things they wouldn't normally do.

There are different levels of possession. Most often the person is oppressed as opposed to possessed. There are also the people who are Perfectly Possessed. Perfectly possessed people have been totally taken over by the invading spirit or spirits and their own personality has disappeared. They are in full cooperation with the demon possessing them.

The only time one could be absolutely sure a person is possessed is when they admit to it and seek help.

If a Catholic priest is called upon he must do a number of consultations with a psychiatrists about the supposed possessed person. The psychiatrist must be able to definitely state that the person is not mentally ill and that therefore, there is no known cause for the behaviour of the person they are assessing.

The priest must then get the permission of his bishop to carry out an exorcism. The reason for this is, that the priest must observe "obedience" You see Satan refused to obey God by accepting Jesus Christ so the priest must put himself firmly in obedience to God.

But what if you have a strong feeling that "there is more than one at home." For instance if you suddenly catch sight of being watched by a stranger out of the eyes of the psychopath. Though fleeting, it is a blood curling moment. There are other moments when your eyes are transfixed to their eyes. They speak in low tones, perhaps only one word. That word lies in your subconscious until later it surfaces and you find yourself thinking or acting in a way you don't want to.

Pray for The Narcissist or Psychopath? You must be Joking!

As Christians we must be obedient to the Master. He told us to, pray for our enemies and do good, to those who hate us.

The prayer for our enemies is of course, **"Lord bless them and change me"**. Many people want to pray: "Lord bless me and change them." By the way – you must use their name! Actually that's the bit I have the most difficulty with.

Now a Psychopath/Narcissist cannot change. If you show them the error of their ways and they promise to change – they will: They begin exhibiting another type of despicable behavior; equally as ugly but you won't be ready for the new stuff.

Take it from me, as one who has suffered to the point of nearly losing my mind; you want God to change YOU. That's the prayer – **"Lord change me."**

Now why do I have to ask God to bless that evil, vicious, malicious, spiteful, predator? Let me explain:

On the cross Jesus prayed: "Father forgive them for they know not what they do." Now although the Narcissist does indeed know what they are doing. They get their pleasure out of watching us suffer. They feed off our frustration, our anger, our bewilderment. They have no conscience, they do not feel empathy: they cannot love. So although they know they are doing wrong and they like it, they have no aptitude to experience the array of feelings that make us human.

This is something we must never let out of our mind. They do not feel. Don't think, "Well of course he or she will not do *that*" or "Of course they will think *this* or *that*." No. No. they won't because you must understand it's just not part of their brain. It's not there.

The: "Lord bless them…" will help you forgive them. Remember you are not blessing their behaviour. This is what happens:

Blessings will return to you:

1 Peter 3:9 "Not rendering evil for evil, nor railing for railing, but contrariwise blessing, for unto this are you called, that you may inherit a blessing." In many places

the Bible tells us that if we bless someone and the blessing is not accepted it will return to us as a blessing.

OR

Romans 12:20 "But if thy enemy be hungry, give him to eat; if he thirst, give him to drink. For, doing this thou shalt heap coals of fire upon his head."

See what I mean!

The Lord Change Me Prayer for the Narcissist actually means, "Lord bless him or her with a conscience, make them realise and feel for themselves the terrible devastation they have wrought in my life. Bring them to their knees in humble, honest repentance."

For our part the Lord Change Me Prayer actually means, "Lord give me the strength to break with this person and never, ever, ever, contact them again as long as I live".

Or maybe you cannot leave. You have to stay for the sake of children. Or you have nowhere to go. Or you are ill or just emotionally weak. The prayer then means:

"Lord change me and show me how to unhook my emotions from this person. Teach me how to shop caring what they think of me. Call to me Lord, that I may only talk to you about my feelings, emotions, my cares, hopes and dreams, so that they know nothing

about me. So they cannot feed of my emotions or get delight in controlling me"

Perhaps we victims of psychopaths and Narcissist don't need God to change us as much as to re-form us.

You see the psychopath might not be human. But we are not like other people either. No. Unfortunately we are the total opposite of the psychopath or the satanically possessed.

Huge research has been done to gather information and understanding on how people become victims of the psychopath. So many people get drawn into their web of deceit and end up totally traumatized, or murdered that counselors have realized that there is a need to warn the public.

Research shows that we victims are not like other people. While normal people's emotions and attitudes ebb and flow gently, ours go off the rector scale.

WE don't have empathy – we have HUGE empathy. Counselors describe it as "high levels of empathy." We are not just loyal – we would die for the Narcissist in our lives – really, honestly die for them. One of the synonyms of "loyalty" is "submission". Wow! Apparently unlike others who have trust, we have Blind Trust. Apparently we are "highly invested in cooperation."

When we look back, recognize and apply these character traits to the situations we were in or are still in – it's shocking, frightening and embarrassing.

When I first came across this report it was on a youtube video which while I was watching my husband was listening to. I was shocked at the content and deeply embarrassed as I recognized myself. I said to him. "Does that remind you of anyone?" He looked at me and gave a little smile. I said: "I'm not safe to be let out!" He said: "I've been telling you that for years."

So when we pray **Lord Change Me.** We now recognize that, it is indeed us that needs, changing

The Prayer is "Lord bless ……. And change me"

We might wonder how we can *do good* to those who hate us. As Christians we have been taught that it is the greatest act of Charity to admonish the sinner. Well that's not such a great idea when dealing with the Narcissist. They feed on conflict.

Instead we need to curtail their evil behavior which is an offence to God and a scandal to others.

To curtail it we cease to be emotionally involved with them. To prevent our emotions getting in the way, begin today to use a whole arsenal of prayer tactics.

"God has delivered me from the domain of darkness and transferred me to the kingdom of His Beloved Son, Jesus." (from Coll.1:13)

I have twice now had to *pray for a Narcissist* to leave my life. The first person had caused the murder of another and got away with it. I prayed that this person would leave the country, so afraid, I was of them. It took seven years of constant storming heaven. God did answer my prayer and that answer has given me great faith and hope. Why did it take so long? Well I had stipulated that they leave and never return so of course that took a bit longer for heaven to arrange. This particular psychopath had to run from the drug barons to whom they owed money. This person won't be back! (sorry for the awkward use of the non-pronoun)

Beware the Love Bombing

Love bombing is usually done at the beginning of a relationship. However if you are trying to escape from the N or P, and they are trying to win you back you will probably be on the receiving end of this type of behavior.

There is quite a bit written about love bombing and describes it as flattery to an excess, suffocating attention by phone, email, text and turning up at your family and friends house.

Eccles: 7:6 "It is better to be rebuked by a wise man, than to be deceived by the flattery of fools."

1 Thess 2:5 "For neither have we used, at any time, the speech of flattery as you know." Saint Paul here shows that flattery is a form of manipulations. He does not manipulate them to listen and accept Jesus Christ.

On the first occasion you try to sort out your relationship with the Narcissist, you will probably be swept along and think that the person has seen the light and realizes that their behavior has caused you pain. How could such a loving sincere person knowingly hurt me, you reason? And you succumb to another dose of the same horrible treatment.

I have just come through a love bombing session. The first fifteen minutes I was thinking "I'll have to go back!"

Then I put my prayer into practice and slowly, slowly the warm fuzzy feeling died down and I was facing a void without feeling.

The Psychopath, (actually I think this one is Satan himself) played every card in the pack. There was one point when his logic began to win me over as we discussed common interests. He played his final card as he was leaving – he looked so vulnerable as he scooped up my little dog and looked at it with such kindness. Like a gentle man, full of feeling and care he reached out to hand me the dog. My heart went forward…. And then I heard a little voice in my head say, "You're the guy wanted to poison your cat. You're the guy who walked right over the top of my friend's children playing in front of you. You're the guy who loves to twist the emotions of little kids and send their parents into a rage – and you got pleasure out of doing it." So I stood still with my arms folded and he had to put the dog down to leave.

Never in my life have I been that strong. If I had I would never have got into a relationship with a person with Narcissistic Personality Disorder in the first place.

We must ask ourselves how we were taken in by the love bombing. How did we allow ourselves to be so overwhelmed?

It was vanity and pride of course. Two vices intrinsically woven into the fabric of every human being alive. Some of our pride was tethered to the satisfaction we felt, that others would know how much we were loved by this new person in our lives. Perhaps we suffered from low self-esteem. Funny thing, low self-esteem. It is a sort of inverted Pride.

Our first love, should always be God. We should love Him with all our heart, our soul, our mind and our strength. Everyone and everything, falls into its rightful place after that.

Mostly we do not realise that the flattery is over the top because the Narcissistic person is very good at it. They watch us. They listen to us. They find out what makes us tick. They uncover our vulnerability. Then they move in. When they find out what we want they tell us they have exactly what we want. They shine like a soul mate.

Is it Narcissist or Demon Possessed?

It is not always easy to differentiate between the NPD (or Narc) and the demon possessed person unless you have come up against both types.

I am of the opinion that the person with narcissist personality disorder can be clinically assessed to some degree. Their personal relationships function on the level of mental and spiritual degradation and abuse of other human beings and yet those same human beings would describe the narcissist as being 'non-human'.

A friend of mine told me that, she had ended her short relationship with her boyfriend. She said he had become angry she saw "someone else looking out of his eyes." Lucy girl. Narrow escape.

If a person is possessed or obsessed by an evil spirit there is something of the original person still functioning while the satanic spirit resides in the individual. Their individual personality can still be accessed. You can still remonstrate with the person. They themselves will know that there is something unwanted driving them to do the things they do. These people can get help through exorcism.

I once worked as a social worker with a young man who would do awful things and immediately afterwards stand shocked and even bewildered at his own behaviour. He would be normal then suddenly in a rage smashing expensive equipment. Then nothing - Normal again. One night after it took six police men to hold him down one of them said to me: "That one's not human you know." This young man will never get help because his family would freak out at the mention of God not to mind Satan.

The Narcissist will blame everyone else for their wrong doing. Or they will "gaslight" you. Or they will lie and twist their way out.

Should you point out their faults the Narcissist being cornered, promise to change – they will probably change that set of behaviours you are addressing but then use another set of unacceptable stuff instead.

Psychologists and psychiatrists argue about wither or not the Narcissus Personality Disorder can be changed or not. Most agree it **cannot** be changed for the better.

However if you have watched Mr Sam Vaknin's you tube channel, you will see that all things are possible.

The Perfectly Possessed however definitely cannot be changed. You cannot pray for them. In fact it is dangerous for you to do so. They will send a spiteful demon after you to inflict a wound on you. The wound will be emotional, spiritual or mental. .

They will not be happy until someone is dead. They will covertly encourage someone to commit suicide. Suicide is known to the Satanist and Luciferins as the eighth sacrament. For them it is an acceptable religious right.

The Perfectly Possessed rarely gets their hands dirty by carrying out a murder themselves. They get others to do it for them. I have personal experience of this type of person. And he did get away with the crime.

The New Testament tells us never to pray for an evil person, never to wish them God Speed.

Your prayer for dealing with the Perfectly Possessed is at all times Prayer for Protection for yourself and your loved ones.

Use the Psalms. Pray them from your heart. Mean every word you read. Apply them to your situation as you read.

Pray This Psalm

Psalm 139 In the Catholic Bible.
Psalm 140 in the Protestant Bible.

Save me, LORD, from evildoers;
keep me safe from violent people.
They are always plotting evil,
always stirring up quarrels.
Their tongues are like deadly snakes;
their words are like a cobra's poison.
Protect me ,LORD, from the power of the
wicked;
keep me safe from violent people
who plot my downfall.
The proud have set a trap for me;
they have laid their snares,
and along the path they have set traps to
catch me.
I say to the LORD, "You are my God."
Hear my cry for help, LORD!
My Sovereign LORD, my strong defender,
you have protected me in battle.
LORD, don't give the wicked what they

want;

don't let their plots succeed.

Don't let my enemies be victorious

make their threats against me fall back

on them.

May red-hot coals fall on them;

may they be thrown into a pit and never

get out.

May those who accuse others falsely not

succeed;

may evil overtake violent people and

destroy them

Look at other Psalms to see if they resonate with your particular situation. Never forget to thank God in anticipation for His help. Be careful about curiosity. Evil can be memorizing.

The Protestant King James Bible and the Catholic Douay Rheims Bible say it best:

"As a dog returneth to his vomit, so a fool returneth to his folly." Probverbs 26:11

Applied to this situation is translates into: 'get away and stay away.'

All over the internet you will see: No Contact! No Contact! Definitely No Contact!.

The Psalms have a particular spiritual power. Composed by King David they have been prayed for two thousand years by holy monks through the nights and days as an unending cry to God from mankind.

If you become really frightened call quickly on God to send Michael the Archangel sword in hand to defend you. Revelation 12: 6-8: *"And there was war in heaven: Michael and his angels fought against the dragon; and the dragon fought and his angels, prevailed not; neither was their place found any more in heaven."*

Sometimes with the Perfectly Possessed you will catch "something" going across their eyes from their left eye to the right. Like something at the back of their eyes. You will be left with the impression of an inner eye lid and you will probably convince yourself you imagined it. You won't dare tell anyone in case they think you're mad. But someone recently has told. A Journalist who stands up for the pre born witnessed this happening in the eyes of the woman who sells the baby parts of aborted babies. And he was not afraid to write about it.

The possessed person will always have an aversion to something religious. I was put off guard recently by someone who I suspected of being possessed because they seemed so religious. Then one day they said to me: "You don't have to read the Bible you know." Afterwards when I thought about it I realised that many of my friends had been advised the same way by this person. We should make a commitment to read the New Testament each day. Ask Jesus to speak to you personally, then open the New Testament at random. Read and pray what He wishes to draw your attention to that day.

Also remember what Jesus promised that whoever, knocked on the door of His heart and asked in His name for help He would never turn them away.

Speaking to your personal angel guardian: "Oh Angel of God, my guardian dear. To whom God's love, commits thee here. Ever this day be at my side, to light and guard, to rule and guide."

Speaking to Archangel Michael "Michael, Michael of the morning, fresh cord of heaven adorning: Keep me safe today and in temptation drive the devil away." (check the internet for the story behind this prayer)

Unhooking Through Prayer

When dealing with a person with any of the Cluster B disorders **<u>Narcissistic Personality Disorder</u>**, Antisocial Personality Disorder, Histrionic Personality Disorder and Borderline Personality Disorder we must be very aware of their desire to manipulate and control us.

A favourite trick of the disordered person is to use their voice to manipulate, cajole and mind control their intended victim – that's you and I.

In one respect we need to listen very carefully for words that don't quite fit in their sentences. Those words are intended to slip into our subconscious and activate at a later date.

In another respect we need not to listen and instead pray as they are talking.

Lots of people are using this technique nowadays. I notice the wholefood practitioner I use did it. He said, "Don't worry about writing down what I say now you will remember everything later" and sure enough a few days later when I was physically occupied with some menial task his advice came flooding into my head!

If the person using this type of mind-control is for our good then we don't have to worry too much about it.

Another way these people operate is to wash you with words until your brain becomes fogged. In this case we need to use prayer for protection.

Pray against the Manipulator

1. Begin on your own to center on God. Either God within the human heart or on God in heaven. You must learn to do this at a moment's notice.
2. Say the "Our Father" – "Lord's Prayer" silently and with great focus while the evil intentioned person is speaking.
3. Let the expression on your face be of *pretended* interest. You could nod, now and again.
4. If the complete prayer is too much or you are expected to make some answer to your opponent then simply keep repeating to yourself, "...*deliver us from evil; deliver us from evil; deliver us from evil.*"
5. Remember you must be totally focused on the prayer.

If the person is possessed the evil entity within him or her will recognize a human praying and become angry, patiently angry and begin to plan retribution.

If the person is your religious leader they are very likely to recognize your face at prayer and they will feel your rejection.

Remember we are choosing God above these cretins, which if we had lived our life in this mode up until we met them; we would not have got ourselves into this situation.

If this is a parent we are dealing with we need to check our own behavior patterns which we may have picked up from them through the years. If Catholic, find a "proper priest (few and far between nowadays) and go to confession! Jesus told His apostles: "Whose sins you shall forgive they are forgiven them, whose sins you shall retain, they are retained." If the priest tries to negate the severity of your sins – get away from him and find another. If you are a Protestant you need to get down on your knees and humbly (out loud) confess your sins to God and ask His forgiveness, telling Him that you mean never to do that wrong again. God forgives seventy time seven so when you fall again like your Catholic brother or sister get down on your knees and confess again. We are human.

To unhook from the Narcissist or evil person, our constant little prayer should be: "*Lord, Thy will be done. Lord thy will be done.*" Seek to learn as much as you can about yourself as the predator highlights your emotional needs. Where are you hurting and why. Speak to God often, at odd times during the day and as you lie awake at night. Address Him as "*Divine Wisdom*", you will be surprised at what you learn about yourself and your need for deep healing.

Now is the time to make a good friend of the Holy Ghost or Holy Spirit.

Prayer to the Holy Spirit

"Breathe into me, Holy Spirit,
that my thoughts may all be holy.
Move in me, Holy Spirit,
that my work, too, may be holy.
Attract my heart, Holy Spirit,
that I may love only what is holy.
Strengthen me, Holy Spirit,
that I may defend all that is holy.
Protect me, Holy Spirit,
that I may always be holy."

Prayer for Protection

<u>Spirit of love and truth</u>, surround me and keep me safe

<u>Spirit of wisdom and understanding</u>, show me how God wants me to get out of this situation.

<u>Spirit of counsel and fortitude</u>, teach me God's plan for me.

<u>Spirit of knowledge and piety</u>, teach me how to keep closer to God for my greater protection.

<u>Spirit of the fear of the Lord</u>, cut this human fear out of my life

<u>Spirit of grace and prayer</u>, teach me how to pray in every situation.

<u>Spirit of peace and meekness,</u> teach me how to rely on God for all my needs

As Christians we know that the Holy Spirit is God the third person of the Blessed Trinity. The above prayer to the Holy Ghost is based on a recognized pattern of prayer and adoration. The first addresses in each line defines the attributes of God. The second part of the prayer in each line can be changed to suit your own particular needs. In Ireland long ago this type of prayer was called a Lorcia.

Prayer

Against

Evil

Witchcraft

Satanism,

I arise today
Through a mighty strength, the invocation
of the Trinity,
Through a belief in the Threeness,
Through confession of the Oneness
Of the Creator of creation.
I arise today
Through the strength of Christ's birth and
His baptism,
Through the strength of His crucifixion
and His burial,
Through the strength of His resurrection
and His ascension,
Through the strength of His descent for
the judgment of doom.
I arise today
Through the strength of the love of
cherubim,
In obedience of angels,
In service of archangels,
In the hope of resurrection to meet with
reward,
In the prayers of patriarchs,
In preaching's of the apostles,
In faiths of confessors,
In innocence of virgins,
In deeds of righteous men.

I arise today
Through the strength of heaven;
Light of the sun,
Splendor of fire,
Speed of lightning,
Swiftness of the wind,
Depth of the sea,
Stability of the earth,
Firmness of the rock.
I arise today
Through God's strength to pilot me;
God's might to uphold me,
God's wisdom to guide me,
God's eye to look before me,
God's ear to hear me,
God's word to speak for me,
God's hand to guard me,
God's way to lie before me,
God's shield to protect me,
God's hosts to save me
From snares of the devil,
From temptations of vices,
From everyone who desires me ill,
Afar and near,
Alone or in a multitude.

I summon today all these powers between me and evil,
Against every cruel merciless power that opposes my body and soul,
Against incantations of false prophets,
Against black laws of pagandom,
Against false laws of heretics,
Against craft of idolatry,
Against spells of women and smiths and wizards,
Against every knowledge that corrupts man's body and soul.
Christ shield me today
Against poison, against burning,
Against drowning, against wounding,
So that reward may come to me in abundance.

Christ with me Christ before me, Christ behind me,
Christ in me, Christ beneath me, Christ above me,
Christ on my right, Christ on my left,
Christ when I lie down, Christ when I sit down,
Christ in the heart of every man who thinks of me,

Christ in the mouth of every man who
speaks of me,
Christ in the eye that sees me,
Christ in the ear that hears me.

I arise today
Through a mighty strength, the invocation
of the Trinity,
Through a belief in the Threeness,
Through a confession of the Oneness
Of the Creator of creation

This is known as the Lorcia of St Patrick and has
been used by Christians for 1,500 years. St Patrick
lived around the year 350 AD. When he came to
Ireland the whole land was Pagan. They used every
type of witchcraft against him. He made Christians
of every one of them. Today Ireland longs to be
Pagan again. All the historical societies do their
best to erase his name and highlight paganism
instead.

But I promise you this prayer is powerful and just
what we need in this New Age Pagan world. Say it
in the morning applying it to your personal
predicament.

The Trinity is the most important piece of doctrine
of the Christian faith.

Our Christian Doctrine:
Is the Father God?

Yes the Father is God and the first Person of the Blessed Trinity

Is the Son God?

Yes the Son is God and the second Person of the Blessed Trinity.

Is the Holy Ghost God?

Yes the Holy Ghost is God and the third Person of the Blessed Trinity.

There are Three Divine Persons in the One God. Father, Son and Holy Ghost.

If you are a Christian you are bound in faith to believe the following:

Jesus Christ is God.

Jesus Christ has TWO natures,

one human and one divine.

Jesus Christ is one person with two natures. .

The total amalgamation of the two natures in

Christ is termed:

"The hypostatic union."

"And glorify thou me O Father with thyself with the glory which I had before the world was, with thee." John 17 v 5.

"In the beginning was the Word, and the Word was with God, and the Word was God." John 1v1

Gas lighting and Lies

Gas – lighting and the telling of lies are an integral part of the equipment of the Narcissist, the Psychopath and the Demon possessed.

Lying is as natural as breathing to a psychopath. It is the overwhelming results of this that leave their victim in such distress. Unfortunately for the victim they are very likely to be extremely trusting people and will be more easily duped than other people might.

When the Narcissist's lies are exposed they do not flinch. They do not blush they simply tell more and more lies to keep you dealing with the fresh information. While you process "how wrong you were about them", your mind turns and accepts the new "picture" of your life, which is all lies. Lies and deception hurt you mentally and spiritually. The mental issues arising from the psychopathical lies, leave you unsure of yourself, with feelings of vulnerability, they lower your self-esteem.

Our lives should be built on a strong foundation. There should be beauty and truth in our relationships. Maturity should be a corner stone of how two people relate to each other. Where there are lies and deception there is only filth, darkness, shadows and hell.

When dealing with these liars one must first clean up one's own act first. There are no half measures here. Refuse to do anything that you might have to tell a lie about afterwards. There is no such thing as a white lie. All lies steal the truth from someone else.

Where lies and truth are concerned there is only black and white. There is NO GRAY.

Satan's first weapon is deception and TRUTH is the best defense against it. Satan is the father of lies (John 8:44). Truth is never our enemy it is our Liberator. Jesus has promised, "The truth shall set you free."

Once you know the truth about whom you are dealing with you can begin to ... your life.

Prayer -Truth in Your Life

Holy Spirit, I adore you as the Third Person of the Blessed Trinity. You are the Spirit of Truth, love and holiness, proceeding from the Father and the Son and equal to Them in all things. I adore You and love You with all my heart. Teach me to be truthful. I have suffered from other people's lies and deception. Holy Spirit, there is only Truth in you. Come into my heart

now and bring the beauty and purity of your Truth to light my mind and my heart. I was created by God. I was created for God in whom there is no deception. Teach me to live for God. Forgive my own lies. Many times I have not told the truth, I have avoided it or acted a lie. Spirit of the Living God, fall afresh on me.

Prayer Against Fear

The Bible lists words "**fear not**" 274 times.

Here are a few of these kindly and sustaining words:

Isiah 41:10 "**Fear not** for I am with thee: turn not aside, for I am thy God: I have strengthened thee, and have helped thee ..."

Genesis 15:1 "the word of the Lord came to Abram by a vision, saying: **Fear not** Abram, I am thy protector ..."

Exodus 20:20 "And Moses said to the people: **Fear not** for God is come to prove you and that the dread of Him might be in you, and you should not sin."

Matthew 10: 29-31 "Are not two sparrows sold for a farthing? And not one of them shall fall on the ground without your Father. But the very hairs of your head are all numbered. **Fear not** therefore: better are you than many sparrows."

Mark5:36 "But Jesus having heard the word that was spoken saith to the ruler of the synagogue: **Fear not**, only believe."

Mark 6:50 "And Jesus said to them: Have a good heart, it is I, **Fear not.**"

Prayer I
"Heavenly Father, I am so afraid. Sometimes the fear brings on terror as I think of terrible things that could happen to me.
It seems, that there is a huge black mountain in front of me. Sometimes it is a long tunnel.
Father you know that sometimes I seem to overcome the fear. I think it has gone away. Then it comes back with a force worse than before.
Please help me.
Now, I am just going to look up for a few moments and focus on You.
Only You Father God.
Only You.

Prayer II

Father God I need a special type of courage now. I don't think I have ever needed it before. It is the courage to *"not care"*. There are things said about me behind my back. Harsh words. Lies. Things I have said, are carried back to my enemies. I feel angry. I cry, sometimes in sadness and sometimes in anger. How did life get like this? How did I misjudge people and situations? Please Help me Father.

Now, I close my eyes Father and "see" into my heart. As I gently breathe, I recall the words of your apostle Paul,
"In You I live,...and move,...and have my being."
(Acts: 17:28)
For the rest of the day my dearest Father I will recall and say these words in my heart. I will relax, even when I am working, and knowing that You, Father, are at the centre of me, I will with Paul say:
"In You I live and move and have my being."

Mark 8:34 "And calling the multitude together with his disciples, he said to them: If any man will follow me, let him deny himself, and take up his **cross** and follow me." Jesus expects us to suffer. He knows that we will carry many burdens. This is God's will for each of us. In these sufferings if we deny ourselves anger, revenge and especially the self-pity and instead accept this horrible

time as a Cross from the hand of God. Carry it willingly
with Jesus as He carried His cross.

Matthew 27:32 "And going out, they found a man of
Cyrene, named Simon. Him they forced to take up His
cross." God shows us very clearly: help my Son Jesus
carry His cross.

Galations 2:19 "…with Christ I am nailed to the **cross**"
Jesus knew what it was like to suffer mentally. During
His prayer in the garden, all His friends instead of
keeping Him company, fell asleep. When one of His best
friends Judas led His enemies to Him, He was deeply
wounded. As totally God, Jesus knew that all this must
happen and as totally Man He suffered. Jesus appeared
before the multitude and they cried crucify Him. He
stood lacerated from whip wounds, He had branches of
thorns bound around His head. His enemies were
delighted. They were laughing at him. They hated Him.
They wanted Him harmed. They wanted Him dead.
They were seething with jealously and envy.

Collossians 1:24 Now I rejoice in my sufferings, … and
in my flesh. I am filling up what is lacking in the
afflictions of Christ …"
Saint Paul knew, because he was taught by Jesus
Himself, that in some way Jesus had left a space for us to
fill. If we willing accepted our suffering and offered

them back to God together with Jesus suffering on the cross, our unhappiness and pain would be transformed into a resurrection. So let us pray.

Prayer III
Father God, in the name of your son Jesus Christ and through the blood He shed on the cross I offer you my suffering in this terrible situation in my life.

Father God when I think of ....(here recall how you were unfairly treated etc)
I Recall also how your son Jesus Christ my Saviour willingly exposed Himself to such torture for me. I bow my head to your holy will and offer you the suffering and pain that I have experienced.

A little bit of doctrine you may have forgotten:
God is most high. To offend so great a being by breaking His laws is an horrendous affront to Him. If we only knew, that to even turn our face away from Him even for a second, by telling a "white lie" or getting impatient He has the right to squash us flat! So omnipotent is He that we could never do enough to repair the damage we do when we sin or break His laws. No human being could ever pay the price. Heaven was closed to us – the human race - because our first parents chose to break God's laws. We are a criminal race. Only God Himself could pay the price for us. Only God could repay God. "God so loved the

world that He gave His only begotten Son..." And so Jesus who is God and the second person of the Blessed Trinity, stood in between us and Father God. He suffered and payed the price for sin which was so high that if we humans every one, suffered and died a million times over we could never afford to repay the debt of our sins.

Only God Himself was worthy enough to pay the debt Himself for us.

Psalm 69

O God, come to my assistance; O Lord, make haste to help me.

Let them be confounded and ashamed that seek my soul:

Let them be turned backward, and blush for shame that desire evils to me: Let them be presently turned away blushing for shame that say to me: Tis well, tis well.

Let all that seek thee rejoice and be glad in thee; and let such as love thy salvation say always: The Lord be magnified.

But I am needy and poor; O God, help me. Thou art my helper and my deliverer: O Lord, make no delay.

Forgiveness Prayers

Matthew 6:14-15 "For if you forgive men when they sin against you, your heavenly Father will also forgive you. But if you do not forgive men their sins, your Father will not forgive your sins." (NIV)

Colossians 3:13 "Bear with each other and forgive one another if any of you has a grievance against someone. Forgive as the Lord forgave you." (NIV)

Ephesians 4:31-32 "Get rid of all bitterness, rage and anger, brawling and slander, along with every form of malice. Be kind and compassionate to one another, forgiving each other, just as in Christ God forgave you." (NIV)

Matthew 18: 21-22   "Then Peter came to Jesus and asked, "Lord, how many times shall I forgive my brother when he sins against me? Up to seven times? "Jesus answered, "I tell you, not seven times, but seventy-seven times."

Forgiving someone means letting them go. "Don't give them your energy" is a popular saying. Sometimes we hold on to anger as a defence against further hurt.

Our first prayer should be:

Lord teach me how to forgive. Teach me to allow, all the cares of earth and this life, to fall away as I look to you for my peace.

Lord grant me the strength to forgive as you forgave the people who tortured you mentally, physically and spiritually.

Everything I have suffered You suffered too. Help me forgive.

Now the forgiveness Prayer.   Begin with the person's name, we will use "Tom"

"Tom I forgive you. I forgive you in Jesus name and in Jesus name you are forgiven."

Christian Meditation

There is a great deal written on both Christian Meditation and Christian Contemplation. The difference is that in Meditation, we as human choose something from the life of Christ to think upon in a prayerful way. Contemplation on the other hand grows out of Meditation but is divinely infused. In other words God stoops down and picks us up. We go soring off into what Saint Paul describes as the "seventh heaven".

The reason I am advocating Meditation as a way of prayer is that firstly we need to redefine our lives as:- God coming first, because that other person replaced God in our lives, for so long and in so many different ways.

Secondly we want to be able to unhook from the psychopath at any time and in any place. If we learn meditation we will be able to apply its benefits when having to deal with difficult situations. It will be of immense value to us if and when we decide to go "No contact" or want to stop ourselves giving information to "flying monkeys" when they come calling.

1. Meditation usually begins the previous evening when we choose a piece of scripture to meditate on the following morning.

2. Time and place are set aside to concentrate on God.
3. A candle burning will help to make this our sacred space.
4. First thing in the morning we begin by addressing God and humbly asking for forgiveness for our sins.
5. We then adore Him and tell Him how much we love Him and want to love Him even more.
6. We begin to read the chosen piece of scripture. As we go we begin to pray it. We talk to God about it. We imagine the scene taking place. We become part of the story. If even one word penetrates our soul and becomes highlighted for us we follow these thoughts without worrying about finishing the piece of scripture.
7. At some point we allow ourselves to become still in front of God. We have read holy words, we have thought holy thoughts now is the time to listen.
8. Silence. Before the all-powerful God. No thoughts. No watching out for something to happen. Just be. You are the creature God made, just be available. That's all.

Never forget that you are made in the image and likeness of God. You have intellect, memory and will. You are like God because you have a soul or spirit. God is spirit. God dwells in the centre of your being. Love Him for He certainly loves you.

Conclusion

Please remember that the person you are dealing with is not like you. They do not respond to situations in the way you would.

Do not, through pride, think that if you love them enough, or show them how they should act, that they will change. They can't do that. More and more often you will read of them being described by the medical profession as being, "not human". For our society this is very serious and it can also be dangerous for you.

My Lord and my God I remind you that Jesus promised that anything we ask in His name you will grant us and so now in Jesus name I beg you to protect everyone who reads this book. Protect them Father from every evil in Jesus name. Give them strength and courage in the face of all adversity. Let them feel your love and protection. Give each reader Wisdom in all their dealings with unkind people who have hearts of steel and warped minds. Give them Your spirit of Truth Father God that they may see situations as You see them. Bless them Father in Jesus name. Amen.

---

[i] Read more: http://www.dailymail.co.uk/sciencetech/article-3235247/How-spot-psychopath-Measure-head-Men-wider-faces-likely-psychopathic-traits.html#ixzz3ydNWDgL4
Follow us: @MailOnline on Twitter | DailyMail on Facebook

Made in the USA
Las Vegas, NV
10 December 2023

82296423R00036